Song for Each Mood Vol 1

By

Michael Tavon

Disclaimer

The artists I support do not reflect my personal views. I love their music, and that's it. I wish not to be condemned for listening to an artist because of their legal transgressions or personal views. Remember, nobody is perfect. Stay blessed, and I hope you enjoy this collection.

Press Play

Playlist one: 4 Her

After the Storm | Kali Uchis

I know your past was a *storm.*
And your brain still rains the pain
from those eyes
but let me be your calm
after the *hurricane*

I'll bring warmth
to your *cold world*
With my arms wrapped around you
The weather will change
To brighter days,

You'll finally see that
Silver lining you were praying for
When the clouds were too dark

Falling in Love Again| Marvin Gaye

I must admit
thoughts of you been swimming
through my mental
drowning in the clouds
of memories I've shared with you

I adore you from the core of my aorta
water can't control you
as you surf across the ocean's border

Never seen perfection
'til I saw your smile;
Once a listless life
You made it shine
Bright like the skyline
Past five in the morning
I pray to the clouds
that you'll be mine

As of now we are
the best of friends
and that is how it will
end or begin

I hope we take the ladder
up to the sky's matter
Past the stars and create magic

Diamonds and Pearls | Prince

The desire to be someone's everything
creates thoughts of doubt
When you find yourself
alone many nights
You wonder, "why?"

Why doesn't this person want me?
Am I not good enough?
What's wrong with me?

You're a pearl
But they don't appreciate your value
by wasting your time

But remember, it takes a special lover
To appreciate your complexity
Everyone isn't mentally rich enough
To pay attention to your precious love.

GreatDaynMornin/Booty D'Angelo

A waterfall down
Descends from your eyes
Because you feel unworthy of love
But did you know,
You are whole on your own

Strong and graceful
So dry the waterfall
flowing from those weary eyes
Your vision is cloudy
See the light; see it clear

You don't need anyone
To validate the love you exude
Love is you

Stand Still | Sabrina Claudio

Goodnight love
I hope you dream well; in peace

You deserve to rest easy
Those sheets are blessed
because they get to cuddle you
instead of me.

I'm waiting til
I'm within reach again
This distance is driving my fantasies
into a daunting reality.

One day my eyes will land
On that smile
and my heart will be calm,
once again.

Until then, get the rest you deserve
I hope you dream of me the way
I dream of you.

Comforter | Shai

Your shoulders are low,
Lean back, fall into my arms

Let my warmth consume you
As I caress your back
Rest your head on my chest
So you can hear the Candance
Of my heart,
'o how it beats so serenely for you

Your day was hell
But your scent still reminds
Of burning incense

My arms wrapped around the world
Nothing brings my heart more solace
I've been waiting for this moment
Since this morning

Your day was long
Baby, rest in my arms
Where you're free from harm.
I won't let you go

Until your headache is gone

I won't let you go
I won't let you go
I promise I will never let you go

Run to the Sun | N.E.R.D

Think of yourself as the sunrise
Most people won't see you shine
Because they're too busy living
A blinded life

With their eyes closed
Yet you still fulfill
Your purpose each day

That's why you're beautiful
And cherished most by those
Who wakes up early enough
To see you spread joy over the world

I'm ready | Tevin Campbell

Waiting for the perfect time,
Often festers into a moment
that never comes

I held my tongue
Like it weighed a ton
Out of the fear
That my words
Would place a burden
On your heart

So I waited for the perfect time
To profess my deepest thoughts
As I wasted hours on the clock
You fell into another pair of arms

Now all I can do is image
What would've happened

If I told you,
Your presence is like magic,
You make sadness disappear
When you smile at me

Every little thing I do | Soul 4 Real

The way you spin me,
I'm surprised
I'm not left upside down
And dizzy

This sensation you bring
Makes me feel like
I'm floating through air,
Flying through water,

My grey world stopped
Feeling normal
Since your presence
Restored its eternal color

Sunshine | Lupe Fiasco

I prayed to God for a blessing
Then came you
A sailing soul
Searching for a heart to restore

I asked...
'ever mend a broken one before?
Because it's heavy and ready
To be carried, again
It has spent the past few years
in a cemetery, buried away

You said,
"I was put in ya life for a reason,
whether forever or a season,
I'll do anything to help you breathe again."

Then we locked lips for a kiss
Or so I thought
My eyes closed
As you performed CPR
Breathing love into my lungs
So I can exhale

My angel, I thank you
For bringing life into my soul
In 30 seconds, I fell in love,
You're my sunshine

Not Gone Cry | Mary J Blige

Your neglect forced my tears to flow
your tenderness, nonexistent
When I confessed my deepest feelings
You left me on read
As I lay in bed doubting my worth
Wondering if it was my fault
After you double-crossed my trust

Now I'm stuck trying
To fix what you ruined
But I've cried enough in one lifetime
You're not worth the drunken
Nights and sad songs

It's time for me to stare into the mirror
And remind myself
Who the fuck I am

When I need somebody | Ralph Tresvant

Your tears have been flowing
Into oceans lately
Must be hard to stay afloat
The way the waves of life
Come crashing down on you
They swallow you whole
Before you're able to catch a breath

I'll part the sea
If you need to see clearly, again
When the weight of the water
Gets too heavy to carry
Hold on to me,

I'm here to guide you to where
You need to be
I refuse to let you drown

Heaven Can Wait | Michael Jackson

I see a wife in you
but you must live your life
Before that day a white dress arrives
There's a lot about you; you must learn
Lessons you must feel
And scars you need to heal
Before you love again
It would be selfish of me
To hold you back from
flourishing on your own
I'll remain close to admire your growth
Once you blossom bright
I'll provide more light
To complete the process

Until then,
Sprout from the concrete
And if you ever need me
Don't hesitate to call
I'll gently free your stem
If you ever get stuck
That's what friends are for

Since I had you | Marvin Gaye

Since I laid beside you
Nothing compares to the comfort
Of your embrace
Your touch put me in a trance
with sweet dreams

A weekend in heaven
Is what I call it, my angel
I yearn to see you again
don't make me wait too long

But take your time, dear
The anticipation will make it taste sweeter
I daydream of seeing you soon
Don't let it be a lie.
I daydream of your stare
I still hear the echoes of your laughter
Your love is mine
forever and after

A Kiss from a Rose | Seal

You exposed me to something new something strange I didn't know how to feel, but it felt good to see your face light up the way it did. The essence of pleasure I thirst for more. I can't wait to feel you again

May This Be Love | Jimi Hendrix

While she's walking
Through Rain
She kisses the moon
To heal the pain
As the wind drifts her away
She lives in a hurricane
chaos for a home
But remains grounded
For miles and miles
She goes alone
Trying to find peace
in the eye of this storm
Even as it hurts
Her problems seem so small
For she has turned brutal rain
into a majestic waterfall

Talk Show Host | Radiohead

On this stage alone with you
I'll tell you all you need to know
I'll answer every question
With truth and conviction

My secrets and dreams
Will be free for you
to explore, no detours.
I hope you're prepared
For the journey in store.

Ask me what you need to know
I have no shame
I'll expose my truth
For the world to know

I aspire to be the greatest guest
Your talk show has ever had

Teach me | Musiq Soulchild

I promise to give the purest form of love
While showing my naked heart
I won't push you away
My emotions are open
If you're willing to enter

Don't be afraid
And I'll do the same
Something beautiful can be discovered
If we let go of yesterday's gloom
To see tomorrow's sun
Without letting it burn our eyes

Diary | Alicia Keys

vent to me
Air it all out
Holding in the stress
Will only kill you from the inside
Don't be afraid to cry
On my shoulder
I'm here to help you rest

Window | Toro Y Moi

"I'm a mess," she said
Well, my heart tends to
Gravitate towards chaos
The kind that remains gentle
and never reciprocates pain
I know you're a mess beloved
I am too

Therefore, our journey
Has come to the same road
I'm so glad we met there.
Memory Lane was just a shortcut
To our perfect love.

So, tell me you're a mess again
I wanna hear more
Tell me what makes your heartache
I'm glad it's still intact; it didn't break
tell me you're a mess

I'll give you space and affection
I'll take my time with you
You're a mess, a beautiful mess

Could you learn to love | Tevin Campbell

Although unrequited
I still love you, why you ask?
I'm eager to learn.

Still Upper Lip / Mr. Hudson

Heart of a Pisces, Pride of a Leo
My thoughts, my dreams
My art and heart
Influenced by you
But I'm too busy swallowing my words,
And biting my tongue

So, when you speak to me
Like I'm the mirror you seek clarity in
You unleash it all
and I with my ears wide open
No matter how loud
your thoughts may speak
Tell me your secrets
To cope with the pain

whenever
    Whatever
        Wherever
            I'll be here

Although
I'm afraid to convey how I feel
I want you, my dear

I care for you
as a homie lover and friend

Til that day
I'll soak in your pain
From his mistakes
And wait for my turn
I can't wait 'til the day

Your Touch | Ralph Tresvant

I feel so warm when I'm with you.
When you touch me, all pain goes away.
My heart, unguarded
When you hold me
Because there's no way
You would ever let my love fall
You have the touch
As gentle as a cloud
But with the force of a storm
When it's time to protect
What you love
Baby, as a man
Your tenderness is what I need
When the world is against me

I long for your touch
Your touch from heaven
Your godly touch

Self-control | Frank Ocean

Some nights you cry
Dancing to slow songs
Drunk off wine
Then you sit in silence
With sad thoughts

And lost memories of them
When you feel empty
You cling to anything
To feel whole again

Sometimes that anything
is a text from them
Have the self-control to move on
Hurt should not live in your heart no more

Really Love | D'Angelo

Your smile brings light
to my tired eyes

When I surrender my secrets
To your open ears
A beautiful truth is all you hear
You don't judge, so I speak without fear

I yearn for your smile
More than sex from another one
That's how deep my feelings go

It's deeper than the moon's craters
We've created a bond far greater
than heaven's mass
This fire won't soon pass
Our flame will forever last

Liberian Girl | Michael Jackson

My beautiful friend
You came in and made life feel so new
Young at heart, old at soul
The way our vibes intertwine
We must've found love
in another galaxy before

A stargazer, soul amazing
I marvel at you
As if I'm gazing at a golden moon
Too good to be true
So surreal to be next to you

My beautiful friend
My care for you is deep, endlessly
At peace with you by my side
Never leave; continue to grow with me

As we reach for eternal bliss
And connect for a kiss
It would be remiss
If I neglected to say this
I love you my beautiful friend

Send it on | D'Angelo

Your love is a letter
with a coded message.
Send it to me so I can solve
The mystery.

You have all the reasons
In the world to be reserved
Until I earn, until I prove
That I deserve your worth.

Keep it all a secret; let me read it.
Don't be stingy; I need it ~~
Your love is a letter
with a coded message,
and I'm determined to solve
the riddles that live
within you.

Intimate Friends | Eddie Kendricks

A new type of love
I've found with you
Unconditional yet healthy
and formed with the purest intentions
We set the right boundaries
To keep us at peace

You're here for me when in need
And I'm never too far from you
Reciprocity is key

And the passion we make is like planets
colliding; a beautiful mess occurs

My intimate friend
So soft and warm
Even when it's cold,
you still wear your heart on a sleeve

I'm thankful to have you
Now you're a part of me
What we have is too transparent
For the naked eye to see

Only When ur Lonely | Ginuwine

You say you feel alone
Even with me
Either my presence is empty
Or your eyes are too clouded to see

Through the rain they caused
So it's me you call
When you need a shoulder to lean on
After they left you to fall

You hold on to what little is left
Because of memories
That are now shadows of today
Are you addicted to pain?
Do you think chasing is a part of love?
While I'm here standing
Willing to give you my all
You're here with me
Hurting over a pseudo lover
Who belongs to the world

We're both in love
With what we can't have
An overpriced heartache
That will leave a debt too steep
To fall in love again

Selfish | Slum Village

Do I have the right to be selfish
When it comes to you
I mean, you're not mine officially
But mentally, we're meant to be
So I can't fathom you loving
On a man that's not me

You're still free
So I let you fly
Live your life
I won't clip your wings
Even though it hurts
To know you still wish to explore
More territories

I could do the same
But I refuse to share my bed
With a woman who isn't you

I'd rather dream of your affection
Than to lie next to another body naked.

We're more than friends
Less than lovers
And in possession

Of deep feelings for each other

Soon, hopefully
This phase will be put to rest
And you'll come back to the nest

For now, can you blame me
for wanting to be selfish?

Teleport 2 Me | WZRD

You fall asleep next to him
With me on your mind
Why must you abuse
Yourself like this?

Settling for what's convenient
To get a temporary fix
Instead of giving us a chance
We deserve each other you know it

You elude my love
Like prey in the wild
And I continue to chase full speed
Hoping you'd eventually give in

You're too special to waste
Your affection on a person
Sees you as a trophy
In their collection

You deserve to sleep

next to a mind
that dreams of you
and a smile that shines for you
when you wake up

Tonight | Lykke Li

No matter how weary you may feel
Or how bright your smile lights the room
You always find time for me
I'm included in every aspect of your life

The light
The gloom
The chaos
The calm

When you call I answer
I feel special to know
You trust me with every piece
Of your delicate existence
and every inch of your temple

A delicate goddess
I handle with care
You have a heavy heart
And I possess the strength to carry

Hammock | Millionyoung

As your world turns upside down
You stand upright
with your shoulders high
Tears rain from those dreamin' eyes
And you smile with confusion.

Your space, you clean
Over and over
Until you feel at ease.

I watch from the edge of your bed
Feeling useless.
Because there's nothing
I can do to help you feel better

Your family abandoned you
Your cat is infected with worms
Friends drifted out of your life
Like a feather in the wind
We're both high on acid
But trippin' differently

I take your hand and kiss your wrist.
"meditate with me," I say.

You lie beside me;

We close our eyes
And inhale three deep breaths
Then, in another dimension
Our minds are set.

We become one.
Your hand in mine.
Our hearts beat in sync.

Our souls became the same.
My best friend,
we're intimate in many ways.
The outside world
Is too blind to understand.

I'll always love you
My energy is here for you

Hold me Down| Daniel Caesar

I tattoo thoughts of you
on blank sheets
Hoping the ink sticks for a lifetime

Tracings of moments we've shared
Penned in word form
I dedicate to your existence

I want this ink
to leave marks on your
heart after you read
the words I tattooed inspired
by you

I write in pen
These thoughts will never fade
I write in pen
While leaving room
For the memories,
We have yet to make

No whiteout
To cover these mistakes
For we will continue to grow together
No retracing the past
As we will write our futures
For the rest of our natural days.

My pen will ink
tattooed thoughts of you
thoughts of us
feelings of love
Hopes of forever

Playlist Two: The Healing Process

Man in the Mirror | Michael Jackson

The world froze the moment
The news was heard
My heart stopped pumping
When I heard the words
"Michael Jackson is Dead"

Suddenly I was crippled
Fell to my knees
As if I had lost someone who shared
the same blood as me

So I cried and cried
Hoping my tears
Would revive you
I wiped my eyes
Hoping the news was just a bad
dream at night

I cried for a stranger because
Your diamond-like spirit outshined
your physical presence
Which is why I felt you

As if you were always next to me

Since age 5
I wanted to be like you
I could never sing
Didn't possess the rhythm to move
But I knew I wanted to inspire love too

Love was your message
All you got in return was
'*Weirdo*' and molestation allegations
This is why I have trust issues now

Because even
When you give the world your all
It will find a way to tear you down

So I cried and cried
For my biggest muse

Your classic Slick curl
Shiny glove
And leather shoes

I cried and cried
For the man
The world refused

To understand
I cried and cried
For the man
I would never see moonwalk again

Street Lights | Kanye West

My only competition is time
And I'm losing by a mile
I'm still runnin' and running
Til I'm breathless

Feels like I'm chasing
Memories long gone
Reaching for a dream
That's out of touch
Yearning for a future that doesn't exist

I'm focused on everything
but the moment
pleasantly overthinking
About things I can't control
and I'm losing it

My biggest fear is aging too fast
Ironically, I let days slip away
with nostalgic daydreaming and procrastination

Waiting for the perfect moment
has put me in a million-minute debt
I must pay off before I die

I'll get where I need to be
Once I decide to live for TODAY

Nikes | Frank Ocean

"I can't breathe,"
The man begged for mercy
As he got pinned down
Like an elusive hog
running from its bath

As the arm around his neck
Clenched tighter
The spectators were
At a loss for air too

They couldn't believe
The blue-collared murder
They had witnessed
Inside, they all died too.

POLLY | NIRVANA

Reality is sadness
so I stay away from the news.

Sex trafficking/Kidnapping/Gun violence
Rape/ Murder

Is all they cover
Then I discover these crimes
Are being committed under my nose
Around the corner
And not too far away from my home.

I'm tired of feeling hurt,
And now I'm numb to it all.

Sober | Childish Gambino

I'm done; no more
Filling my body with toxins
Hoping my heart
Grows numb to the pain

Booze drowns the truth
When the night is young,
But as time wanes
Dark thoughts
Haunts my heart
Until joy becomes a ghost,

This will be my last swim
In this alcohol river

Once I heal from my hangover,
I'll be better off sober,
It's time to treat my mind and body
With more love

Blackberry Molasses | Mista

Blackberry molasses
Life can taste so sweet
But when you feel too weak
To lift the weight off your shoulders
Remember God gave you,
The strength to endure
Storms and pain

Even when that muscle
In your chest tears apart
And you yearn for it to stop
Give it time to recover,
You'll come back
Stronger than before

Don't let the rainstorms drown you
And when the wind
Makes you stumble
Please, break your fall before
You hit the asphalt
Keep moving

The sun may feel like hell right now
But remember
When sun rays felt like,
Warm silk
On your skin

Blackberry molasses
Sweet moments will come after
Bitter pain remember
To forgive the past
but don't run to it ever again

We All Try | Frank Ocean

Sometimes ignorance comes from a lack of understanding. We're often jaded by what we were raised to believe. Some people never explored life outside of themselves. Instead of responding with rage or arrogance. Communicate through empathy and compassion. Help guide the lost minds with the light of wisdom, not ego.

...because we weren't put on this earth to agree with everything we say or do, but humility is important. We all sin. We all fuck up. We all try. No human is greater than the other. Remember, our purpose is to teach those who are willing to receive, not belittle them.

Hurricane | Bob Dylan

What is it like to be black, you ask?
For starters

Imagine life flashing before your
Eyes at the sight of red and blue lights

You question if this interaction will
End in cuffs or death
It's a blessing to leave alive

Imagine being treated
Like you have skin made of iron,
So when shots get fired,
It takes 22 bullets to take you down

Imagine being a suspect
Of a crime, you didn't commit
Imagine being assumed a threat
Because your skin tone
Has a darker shade

Imagine being hated
and beaten for no reason

Imagine getting your invention

Stolen by a white man and watching
Him get richer as you die slow,

Poor and alone
Imagine being loud, but everyone
Ignores your pain.
That's what it's like to be black

White Manz World | 2Pac

It's not a coincidence,
The mission was to oppress
Black People and women
'They' only wanted to see
Us in the field or a kitchen

For decades we caged in our
Our rage with silence, marching for peace
Despite being killed in violence
'They' tried to strip our identities
Yank out our tongues
Raped of us our pride
Leaving bodies hung

Women gave life
But couldn't have one of their own
Confined in the prison
They called home
~~~
Sixty years later, blacks are still trying
To break away from chains
'They' still see us as monkeys in the wild

Women still demand respect

For their bodies and mind
'They' only see them
~~~

As tools for easy pleasure.
Both parties still seek equal pay
Women still don't feel safe

Living in constant fear
of sexual assault and death

One day this country
Will become undivided
I believe in us
I believe in God
I believe in Love

As long as we continue to push
Forward to the future
The past will slowly become
Memory's afterthought

Complexion | Kendrick Lamar

Most good people
desire to be 'part of something
greater than themselves
Finding purpose is why we breathe
Good people speak up
When they see wrong being done to others
Even when the victim(s)
have no resemblance to them.

Empathy is God's light
That shines within us

Good people are
eager for change
They'll do anything to help
Push societal boundaries over the edge

Ever-flowing motion
is the key to progress

Good people listen to the pain
Voiced by those who've been silenced
For decades
Two ears were given
To receive and understand.

Good people
Accept the flaws, mistakes, and sins
Of their brothers and sisters
Without turning their noses to the sky

We're all born imperfect for a reason.
Above all, good people
Pass their knowledge down
To the blissfully ignorant
Without arrogance

We were put on earth
to teach and love each other

Stand Up | Andra Day

A heart without hope
Is a clock that slowly ticks
Til Father Time arrives.
And a mind without a dream
becomes pink-grey matter flooded
With thoughts of fear or nothingness

Some of us lose the battle

Before putting in the effort to fight
Due to a lack of hope
Or the constant flux with fear.
Instead of giving up
What's there to lose in trying?

"I gave it my all."
Sounds better than,
I should've, I could've, I would've

Just Another Day | Queen Latifa

I'm surrounded by hopeless souls
And abandoned homes.
Section 8 babies,
stray cats and dogs
It's dark every night
Because the city never
Changed the streetlights
~~~

Gunshots serve
as my early morning alarm
The glass of broken
beer bottles scattered
Over the streets
Grass and alleys.

The air is filled with the aroma
Of weed and cheap liquor
This is where I live
The neighbors stare as I walk by
But don't even know my name
Why care to learn who we are
When we barely know ourselves

Living here is a never-ending path
To know where.
Signing a lease is the same
As signing a death certificate here.
~~~

UnPretty | TLC

As insecurity echoes
Through your mind,
Like an empty hall

Fill those vacant spaces
With thoughts of self-worth

Learn new ways to fall in love
With yourself,
Marry the idea of accepting
who you are

Prove self-doubt wrong
You are stronger
Than what you give
yourself credit for

Hallucinating | Future

Late nights with my thoughts
Are often scary
They wander to murky valleys

Even when sober,
I still get drunk off loathing
And high doubt

Hallucinations have me thinking
My cold dark room is a paradise
I don't need drugs to go crazy.
I'll be off the edge if I'm lonely after two am.

I'm fine during the day but
It's hard to love myself when it's this late

I should be used to this,
but I'm not and never will be.
Wish I could go to sleep,

Insomnia is my best friend
And I don't have the strength to resist
When anxiety seduces me.

Shelter from the storm | Bob Dylan

I wish I could be white for a day
So I can be blind to injustice
And enjoy my privilege in peace

I could take a break
from being a suspect
To every pair of eyes,
That's blue and green
And a target to every person
With a gun in a blue uniform

A day I am welcomed by greeters
As I enter a decent store or fancy restaurant
And get the service I deserve.

A day, if I decide to shoot up
A school or church,
I'd remain alive and labeled
as *a nice troubled kid*
or ' man with mental illness.'

Because it hurts to be victimized after your life
gets taken away for being black on a Tuesday
afternoon

It would be nice not to be labeled

as a crime for a day
A day of which, no matter what I do
I could kill an innocent person
Or steal from the poor
I'd still have a higher chance
Of making it home than a black man
Riding a bike to work

And lastly, a day that even if I whisper
Platitudes of nothingness
My voice would still get heard before
The screams of pain and oppression
From people of color

It would be great to be white for just one day.
why can't I be white just for a day?

Pinocchio Story | Kanye West

When you stand toe to toe
With the truth
Will you stand tall or crumble
Will you embrace it or run away?

Will you reveal yourself
or play hide n seek?
Our relationship with the truth
Is unstable

We beg for it from those we love
When it's given, we become defensive
It's even worse when it's time to be real
with ourselves

We elude the truth with vices,
Leaving us hollow
And unfulfilled when we come down.

Just like Pinocchio
We wish to be real
But attempt to avoid the truth
That comes with it

Playlist Three: Nostalgia

Somebody Else | The 1975

I wanted to be lovers
A feeling I refused to suppress
You wanted to remain friends
A feeling that wasn't going to change
We parted ways
Yet and still I yearn to see you again

You say we're just friends
In my heart, we're far more
You refuse to let me go
And I let you come back
Like you never left before

A constant cycle
We keep spinning
A game of hearts
Neither of us are winning

Back in the Day | Ahmad

I remember when I was small
playing ball with my father
now we seem more distant
than an overseas call
I love him and all
but shit is different
no more pancakes and bacon
steaming from the kitchen
I sit and wish and reminisce
about my grandpa, rest in peace
sitting on the porch
watching Tom & Jerry
as I inhaled the 2nd hand smoke
from his lungs, I was young
outside with the old heads, I hung
catching tight spirals from my uncle
before he caught a bid of twenty
now, as I sip Hennessey
I really miss the old me
My old life when being poor was fine
And I was blind to the misery
I was surrounded by.

Honey Molasses | Jill Scott

I once tried to find love
In anyone who was willing
to lay next to me

Trying to turn one-night stands
Into happily ever afters
Was the hopeless romantic
In me, manipulating my mind
Into believing my heart
Could fall for anything
With a smile and a story of pain

I latched onto new women
Month by month
Until my heart was exhausted
Leaving a smoke trail
Of disappointment in the air
Once the smoke cleared, I was left more
damaged than ever before

I used to blame them for running away
Now I see why; it was me.
I tried to force my love upon them
Until they could no longer expand.
I was a fool rushing to be loved
Before loving myself.

Three Cheers for Five Years
| Mayday Parade

Fools fall in love
And I was a fool for you
For a while, I didn't mind
Until my pride arrived to remind me
that I am more than small fish
Sadly swimming through
Your pond

Born & Raised | John Mayer

Never seen love close
To me, it's as real as a UFO

My grandparents slept in separate beds
My parents rarely laughed, hardly hugged
And I never saw them kiss.
The same goes for my aunts and uncles too

They celebrated divorce
More than marriage.
In my family, holy matrimony wasn't
"Til death do us part."
It was death,
Death to the old you,
Death to your old life,
Locked down in monotony,

Clipped wings, no room to fly
I remember watching the Cosby Show
and believing love was only real
in a different world

I once convinced my young mind
Love was only fiction — scripted
And the only bond between two adults
could have in real life was distance
- under one roof –
two people with dead roots

and stunted growth.

Love wasn't part of the bargain
Just the security of being miserable
with another body

Furthest Thing | Drake

We share the same name
But vaguely know each other
We visit on the holidays
But during the year, we never care

Our faults
Our flaws
Our trauma
We laugh them off.

Passive when we speak
aggressive when silent
Every dispute ends in verbal violence
The only common bonds are
Alcohol, depression, gossip and
Empty confessions

Why are we like this
We're getting older
But we still refuse to grow
We ignore our love
Then pretend to mourn
when someone is dead and gone

Recovery | Justin Bieber

I'm used to being alone
I've found comfort and solace
In not being hurt by someone
Who claims to love me

So stay where you are
I no longer need your presence
You'll soon regret ignoring my message
And when you need me don't call
Continue chasing the person
You're longing for
As they neglect you too

I remember | Kodak Black.

I live where hope is scarce
And dreams are farfetched

So I kept my aspirations to myself
As I worked alone
Without support
I knew all I needed was myself

When I tried to express
My family didn't understand
My peers doubted the process
Others believed I wouldn't see it through

I remember the fake grins
And curiosity
I was stuck trying to prove my worth
To those who didn't deserve my time
~~~
Fast forward to my first release
The anxiety, the stress
I thought I wasn't good enough because
Very few cared.

Then came the second, then the third book
~~~

the same results

I thought I wasn't good enough
As everyone scrolled past my posts
I contemplated giving up

I went to work lethargic
And begun to accept the notion
Of being a failure
~~~
An epiphany struck
I didn't give up I kept working
I kept writing until
People heard me
Now the energy is different
People pay attention
~~~
Here's my advice to you
If you believe in your dream
Don't let the outsiders
Discourage what's on the inside of you
Let your heart carry you, not your doubt
Not the pity
Let your drive push you forward
Never let resistance pull you back

Africa | Toto

The rain clears
The thunder goes back to sleep
The sun comes back out
to play with the clouds again.
Even the sky has children

Bad | U2

I was born in dysfunction
Raised in sadness

Surrounded by nothingness
Somehow, I grew up knowing
My destiny was far greater
Than the life
I was given

Even when it seemed
Like I was trapped
By dead ends
I let my faith drive me
To the road less traveled

Now the road to success is clear
I was the only one who believed it existed

Playlist Four: Feels Good to Feel Good

God Gave Me Style | 50 Cent

When my mind was pitch black
And I swallowed self-pity
Along with a shot of whiskey
I loathed in loneliness
So I slept with any woman
Because I was convinced
My love was worthless.

I got high til I forgot
how to feel the emotions I tried to kill
Suddenly, I came to realize
I'll be fine as long god is in my life

I thank Mom for her love
Even when the truth was ugly
She never concealed it like makeup
I love my friends for reassuring
my worth

Taking my pain and turning it to hope
Loneliness was a facade
because I always had my loved
ones by my side

I've learned it's okay to cry
I'll still be strong
and lying to myself
only makes the hurt last longer
And shame is okay if

I'm willing to fix it
and a broken heart
is always ready to be mended again

Neon Dove | Gardens & Villa

I was once afraid of storms
Now I marvel as lightning strikes
And when thunder roars, I cheer
I used to run away from the rain

Now I bask in the madness allowing
The shower to downpour
To wash the fear off my shaking hands
The shower from heaven
Soaks my clothes and skin
Releasing me from yesterday's filth

I am me, once again
Yesterday's fear
Tomorrow's anxiety and doubt
Goes down the drain.
When the rain subsides
Because all I have is now
Which is the greatest reason to smile
I thank the storm for giving me bliss

It Runs Through me | Tom Misch

I used to be broken when I was alone
Now I'm whole since I focused on myself

All I need is me; the love has always been
within. Dwelling in a cave used to be my
domain.

Now I bathe in the sun, carefree with bliss
feeling good feels foreign, but I can adapt
My season is here.

No more holding back
The future is mine. The future is mine
I'm free from loneliness because I have myself.

Kush & Corinthians | Kendrick Lamar

I am humble
I am confident
I am anxious
I am calm
I am normal
I am unique

I am everything but weak

I am loser
I am a winner
I am a saint
I am a sinner
I am a jerk
I am sweet

But i assure
I am everything but weak

I'm a bashful
I am wild

i frown
I smile

Some days I run from the sun
On other days I take the heat

But I promise I am everything but weak

I'm a survivor
I've felt pain
I have fallen
Time and time again
Even at the toes of defeat
I stood tall and proclaimed

I am everything but weak

If I Ever Feel Better | Phoenix

My sadness is past tense
I'm glad it's all behind me
Now, when depression
Calls I hit the dial tone.
I'm not running away
I've just grown
and we don't relate anymore

I took the world off my shoulder
And placed it under my feet
I stand under the shade
Instead of taking the heat
I shine when I smile
It's no longer a facade
Thank God, Thank God
I'm finally fine

All I Have to do is Dream | The Everly Brothers

When it comes to reality
I often like to escape
So I fall asleep
When insomnia stops singing

The moments of peace I receive
When my eyes close is pure bliss

I dream of strawberry fields
and candy rain
Wine-colored clouds and flowers storms

I also dream of racial harmony
Gender equality, aliens,
Reduced depression and love

All may seem like fairy tales
but when I sleep,
they're within sight distance

These are the dreams
I wish to not wake up from
One day these dreams
will come to fruition,
and I'll never have to sleep again

As if you read my mind | Stevie Wonder

Four in the morning
I'm up dreaming about life
The future is bright

Pink + White | Frank Ocean

Laying in a bed of grass
Face to the cotton sky
Smiling wide
Eyes cry from the burning sunshine
Don't mind if I go blind
Everything's fine, everything's fine
~~~~~~
As the earth rotates
I find balance
on this shaky ground
Fear was lost, Love was found
Everything's fine, everything's fine
~~~~~~

Show You the Way to Go / The Jacksons

A nation of peace
Shouldn't be a dream
Because it's possible
If we strive to love
a little bit more each day
It's our purpose

Less selfishness
Less ego
Less vanity

Can we try to have an open mind
with pure intentions
And listen to each other?

I'll never lose faith in us
I hope you still believe
In us too

Pursuit of Happiness| Kid Cudi

This part of my life
Is called not giving up
God has me on hold
But I'll leave a voicemail
Or text
I hope I get a call soon

Time is rushing me to age
But I'll remain young in spirit
And patient with faith.
I won't crack
I won't crack, again

I've had meltdowns
Suicidal thoughts
Giving up seemed logical.
But I can't give up
Even when silence falls
And I convince myself
No one loves me.

Which is far from fact
The pursuit of happiness
Is what keeps me going
I know it's not far away

San Juan Street | Deodato

Sit outside
Let the warm breeze tease you
Observe nature at work
I promise you'll feel better
As the water gently drifts through the rocks
And minnows swim upstream
You sit under the oak tree
to hear a song of peace

Serenity is all around
When you listen
The wind whistles
A pleasant song
The leaves on the tree branches
Join too

Your phone is off
You're disconnected
from the outside world
This is the first time
Your anxiety has parted ways
With you, the weight is off your chest
You can breathe again
You can breathe again
You can breathe again
You have found a haven within you

Optimistic | Radiohead

My outlook
Is the *glass half full now*

Waking up to
The sky filled with orange and blue
The warm sun warm greets me
I dislike caffeine, so music is my coffee

I go to work
The idea of a job still boils my soul but the
Fresh faces of children eager to learn
Makes it worth it
It gives waking up early a purpose

The pay rate is low
I often come home fatigued

with a headache, but it's worth it
~~~ back to the topic
Mondays are the best day
When done right
I love them more than Saturdays
Sometimes Friday too
~~~

After an easy Sunday
Monday morning
Is what I look forward to

Don't Fear the Reaper | Blue Oyster

Felt like my life
Was in flux and retrograde
I couldn't catch a break
Constantly paying for the mistakes
I made - left me in debt
I was hollowed out by the reaper's scythe –

I wanted to die
Now, my soul is light
My heart is full, and my mind is clear
My intentions are pure

Love and support
From my energy Is what I needed

To see the light
I'm happy now

1983... a merman I should turn to be | Jimi Hendrix

Rain is more beautiful than sunshine

I stare at the raindrops
splatting in the grass

The Thunder,
Tells the wild animals to go home

Lighting strikes high
Like fireworks on the 4the of July

The world seems to be more
at peace when it pours.
Everyone runs for shelter

Not I; this is when I go outside.
Mother Nature creates her most beautiful music
amid calm storms and chaos.
I love the rain more than sunshine

Fine Again | Seether

It feels good to feel good again
It's been a long walk to this road
And my soles are worn out
But it was worth it –

I've been through
detours and dead ends
But I kept going
It was worth it –

I climbed the mountains of hell
Which burnt my palms and knees
But I made it to the side
Where it's blue and green
It was worth it –

I was down but hopeful
That gave me the strength
To push forward
The travel was turbulent
I was losing my balance
But I found a few shoulders to lean on
And it made me feel less alone

I'm thankful for it all
And it feels good to feel good again

Overjoyed | Stevie Wonder

Rain is synonymous with pain
Because flowers bloom from sky showers

Here is a list of ways
These beautiful elements are the same.

Rain is beautiful when you listen for the
Calmness behind the thunderstorm

Pain is beautiful when you grow
from the trauma and harm

Pain and rain bring life
Pain and rain help us reflect at night

Pain and rain
Will have you runnin' for shelter
Pain and rain
Will often leave you feeling Helpless

After a storm
After a heartbreak
There's always a lesson learned
And room for growth

Pain and rain
Are the twins birthed by mother nature
And father time

Hard to tell em apart
When your heart is broken

Hard to see the beauty
That comes from both
When your eyes are closed

Pain and rain are so beautiful
When you survive the chaos
They often bring

Playlist Five: late Night Action

Come and Go With Me | Teddy P

Your lips taste like the wine
You've been sipping
now I'm drunk off your kisses
assume the position
And prepare for what your body is missing

With your back arched like
a crescent moon
Hope I don't erupt too soon
gotta keep my cool
As you move those hips
The way you do

Once we achieve our releases
I kiss one of your cheeks
to say thank you for this special pleasure
what you have down there
is a treasure

Come and Talk to Me | Jodeci

You stare heavy because you're ready
To feel all my love inside
But before i begin
The anticipation must build

So I mount on top,
and wine between your thighs
Close your eyes, baby
And imagine
What gonna do to you

I kiss and lick your erotic zones
One by one
Til I'm down to your panty line

There's wetness around your island
I'm ready to sail in the motion

You're floating already
Those moans
As I tease you down, there strokes my ego
Before I'm stroking in you

You gasp sensual pleasure
As my tongue searches for your pearl
Then you go wild when I find it
I'm drownin' now

Keep your eyes closed
Keep dreamin'
As I make your fantasies come true

No ordinary love | Sade

Fuck the loneliness
Out of me
As I stroke your pain away
This chemistry was created
Because of our past mistakes

I see it by the way your eyes roll
And flutter
I can see it on your face
No man has
Given such tenderness,
comfort, power with each stroke,

...And
The way you
Get on top

And take the throne
Displays the queen you are

You wind your hips
So I can get deep inside

you make me submit to you
I love it
I fucking love it

Everything about this connection

Feels like destiny
We were meant to forget
Our pasts, through passionate
aggressive lovemaking

Conversations in a Diner | DVSN

So many pieces of you
Others weren't patient enough
To put together, so they left you
Scattered like an unfinished puzzle.
They saw the challenge as
Too time-consuming and difficult

I must say
You're well worth the wait
I'll stay up
Til 3 am to figure you out

The complexities of your love
Sparks the light within me
That wants to learn every little thing

You're 'difficult' for a reason
Your love isn't for beginners
you're far from simple
I appreciate that part about you

So give me all pieces to you
And I'll give my best effort
To solve the puzzle of your heart

Thursday | The Weekend

Under these sheets
We've created a new song
with the rhythm of our motions
and the harmony of our moans
I wrap a hand around your neck
and take a piece of your soul
Sing your heart out
As I go deeper than a tenor
But I'm still gentle when I enter
Pacify my breath
with your breasts
They taste like cinnamon
As I strive to help you arrive
I pull your hair
And stare into your eyes
You latch onto me
Baby, Please don't let go

Touch Me, Tease Me | Case

Be my FaceTime pleasure, my cam girl fantasy
Strip down to your panties
Then dance carefree

I'll be your number-one fan
As I marvel at your bare skin

Make me wish I was there
Make me yearn for your touch more

You move along as the song plays
Flailing your hair, twirling your hips

So comfortable you are
As phenomenal as you can be

Tease me without touching
Allure me without the scent

Connect | Drake

Before our bodies aligned, our minds
intertwined, creating a universe of our own
The love we made shifted planets
And set stars to flames.

Sweetest Taboo | Sade

When you scream, moan, and whisper
My name
It's music to my ears
I put it on repeat
again, again, and again
Say my name
Sing it from your diaphragm
Let it echo off the walls
Say my name, say my name
Say my name baby
Say it to my face
Say it to my shadow
Say it to the wind
To let the earth know
It sounds sweeter every time

Say Yes| Floetry

Coming down from a sex high
Suffering from withdrawals
And hot flashes

Missing the taste of your lips
The melody of your moan
The mesmerizing wind from your hips

The way you dance between the sheets
Left me in a trance

You're a professional
Baby, there's nothing you can't do

You sucked the life from my neck
You took the power
You made it yours, love

You loved me down
Until I reached heaven

Little Red Corvette | Prince

Maybe we're moving too fast
But it feels good
I love the way you ride
When i shift gears
We drive until the gas light
Flashes.

Baby, the speed is just right
And the lane is clear
We can maneuver carefree
And when you get fatigued
Switch from a stick shift to automatic
To make it last

This trip with you is an experience
I will never forget

Voyage to Atlantis | Isley Brothers

On this turbulent voyage
Over vicious waters
That's trying to swallow us alive
We've found a balance
Amongst each other
By holding each other down
The harsh winds may try to set us apart
But we hold each other

Close like we have one heart
I'll never let the motion
Take push you over the edge

And if it ever did, I'll dive in to save you
You won't let me drown

Nor will you allow
the waves to overtake me
You'll take my hand, and I'll grab you tight
As we tread and float
Under the crashing water.
~~~
Never sail away from me
Never sail away from me
If we ever somehow drift away
I promise to find you again
~~~
This voyage called life Is often crucial
But for as long as I have you

And you have I
Vicious waters won't stand a chance
To survive.... against you

Hotel SixNine | Spooky Black

I only want to be alone with you
Away from chaos

The world has a way of making me feel small
But you make me believe I'm larger than life

With those wide eyes
You stare like I'm irresistible
We connect forehead to chest
For a kiss that's strong enough
To heal each other's pain.

Babe, I hope you're listening
To the way my heart beats
The rhythm is inspired by you
I wanna be alone with you
Until we're the last two lovers
On this dying earth.

We can let time pass by
That's fine
Forever seems like a dream
With you

Explosion | Marques Houston

You're gonna erupt

Like a volcano

Once I'm done with you

Leaving your thighs to shake

Causing a quake on the landscape

It's gonna take

A while to clean up after you

Freak N You | Jodeci

Making love to you in the morning
Is a sight to behold

The sun's rays shine
through the blinds
And reflect off your honey skin

We still smell warm
showers from last night,
your hair unkept from me tugging
during backshots

We're wide awake and fully energized
fucking on a full tank of passion
You ride me til the wheels fall off

You're a goddess on top
bold and fierce
I glance at the mirror
It looks like a dream
on a clear screen
Baby, you're so special
Baby, you're beautiful

Call me Papi as you
pounce like a cat
Bite my chest
Clench my neck
I love it

You're a wild one in the morning
Like you're sexually possessed
Making love to you in the am
feels like an out-of-body experience

Shadow Dance - The Internet

Move through the darkness
With your grace and confidence
Natural is your most beautiful state
Your hair, as wild as your spirit
It's fitting you wear it
Like the blue silk nightgown
You're dancing in now

The red wine is kicking in
Sade plays through the speaker
You dance to the rhythm
You dance for me
In the dark

I stare as you shamelessly you
The shadow on the wall
Mirrors your movement
The nightlight
Creates a pretty aura around you

So beautiful and free
A sight to behold
A sight I don't deserve
But God blessed me
With an angel on earth

Distant Lover | Marvin Gaye

You being five hours away
Feels like a year
When you're not right here
When I need you

I miss having you wrapped in my arms
As you caress my hand
Feels like the world is next to me
When we cuddle.

My dreams are more vivid
When we sleep side by side
We become the center of the universe
And our worries disappear
I miss you so, I miss you so bad

Every moment we share
Even when we're silent
I treasure more than the moon

My distant lover
I ***loathe*** when I depart from you
Because I don't know when
I'll see you face-to-face, again

I'll come back soon
I refuse to stay away for
Too long
I promise

Spotless Mind | Jhene Aiko

I always recall
The first time we made love
The intensity created heatwaves
The slow jams played
But you sang louder
Your palm tenderly slapped my back
As we cradled, upwards
In each other's arms
The room was lit by the muted television
screen...It felt like a movie
You whispered in my ear
I have no clue what you said
But it was music
To my soul

Feels so right | Lloyd

How my imagination runs wild
As I dream of your hot skin sticking to mine
Close your eyes so tight
You can feel my hand tracing the wetness
between your thighs

I fanaticize the ways
I'm going to make music with your body

Your moans will sing
Your heart will drum
Your frame will shake
That flower will hum
A pretty melody
As I stroke
Deeper
Faster
Slower
Longer
Side to side

I strum your hair like the strings
Of a Spanish guitar
Before pulling it back
Then massage your shoulders
So you can relax a little
My lovin' gets intense

You deserve every inch
On your stomach, you lay
I get to dig deeper inside
Between those cheeks
A mess you made on the sheets
As we create the beautiful music
We put on repeat

Call to Action

Dear reader, please consider posting a picture of this book to your Instagram feed or story. This small gesture will help this book gain exposure tremendously. Simply tag my account @bymichaeltavon or use #michaeltavon

You may also post a pic via Twitter and tag @michaeltavon

You may also post a review on Goodreads or amazon. Anything helps.